THE JOY OF CHILDREN

For Catherine Montgomery Pearls

Greetings

from

Pearl S. Buck

February
1965

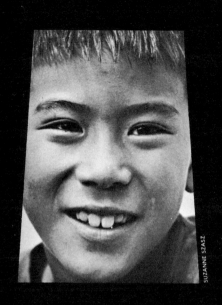

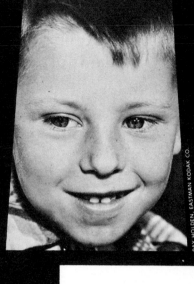

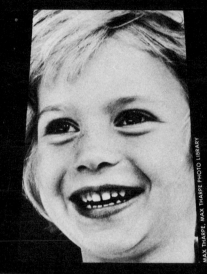

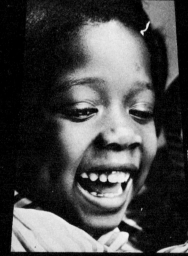

SUZANNE SZASZ

RAY HOLDEN, EASTMAN KODAK CO.

MAX THARPE, MAX THARPE PHOTO LIBRARY

TANA HOBAN, RAPHO GUILLUMETTE

PHOEBE DUNN

MAX THARPE, MAX THARPE PHOTO LIBRARY

THE JOY OF CHILDREN

Text by
PEARL S. BUCK

with an introduction by

ROY SORENSON
Chairman, National Committee for Children and Youth

Based on the photographic exhibit prepared
for the 1960 White House Conference on Children and Youth,
"These Are Our Children"

THE JOHN DAY COMPANY **NEW YORK**

SPECIAL ACKNOWLEDGMENT

THE NATIONAL COMMITTEE FOR CHILDREN AND YOUTH WISHES TO EXPRESS ITS GRATITUDE TO EASTMAN KODAK COMPANY
FOR THE WORK DONE BY THE COMPANY IN ASSEMBLING, DESIGNING AND PREPARING THE PHOTOGRAPHIC EXHIBIT,
'THESE ARE OUR CHILDREN,' FROM WHICH THE PHOTOGRAPHS IN THIS BOOK ARE TAKEN.
THIS EXHIBIT WAS PREPARED BY KODAK AS A CONTRIBUTION
TO THE 1960 GOLDEN ANNIVERSARY WHITE HOUSE CONFERENCE ON CHILDREN AND YOUTH.

INTRODUCTION

The Joy of Children, and its sponsor, The National Committee for Children and Youth, both stem from America's love and concern for children. Once each decade over the past half century, beginning in 1909 with President Theodore Roosevelt, a White House Conference on Children and Youth has expressed that love and concern by mobilizing public and professional effort for a better life for children and youth.

The 1960 White House Conference called by President Dwight D. Eisenhower strengthened this vigorous tradition. Seven thousand people, including fourteen hundred young people, representing every conceivable interest in children and youth, met "to promote opportunities for children and youth to realize their full potential for a creative life in freedom and dignity." The Conference focus was on the effects of our rapidly changing world on the development of the young, on appraising and reappraising the values and ideals we live by and on studying the factors that influence individual fulfillment — family, religion, education, health and community life.

In the preamble to the *Recommendations* from the Conference, John Gardner wrote:

The Conference, stemming from the grass roots and culminating in the White House, is itself an exciting instance of democracy at work. Several million citizens, working through official committees in all states and territories, participated in activities leading up to this meeting. Involved in the preparations was a wide range of public and private organizations, and scientific and scholarly societies. Federal and state governmental agencies cooperated fully, but the Conference was conducted by the people of the United States.

We have recognized the devastating rapidity of change that marks this moment in history. We have sought to understand the impact of this change and to grasp its implications for our future efforts.

But as we must cope with a changing environment, so we must rededicate ourselves to the unchanging values which give meaning to American life. We affirm our belief in the dignity and worth of the individual. We affirm our conviction that each child should be enabled to realize his full potentialities. We believe that this fulfillment of the individual must occur within a moral framework, and that the young person must grow up with a lively sense of commitment to the society which fashioned his freedom.

A photographic exhibit, "These Are Our Children," assembled by the Eastman Kodak Company, was a dramatic part of the 1960 White House Conference. The idea for this book was conceived there. Delegates returned again and again to the photographs and found themselves able to go back to the hard work of the Conference table with rekindled feelings about the young subjects of their discussion. It was not long before delegates were expressing a wish that a means be found to make widely available these memorable photographs of children from birth to maturity — their laughter and tears, their wonder and woe, and their clear-eyed vision of a world which hopefully may become better for their having come into it.

The National Committee for Children and Youth was also born out of the 1960 White House Conference, continuing the relationships between the many state committees, national organizations and Federal agencies for the purpose of implementing the goals, spirit and recommendations of the Conference. This unique organization of government, voluntary organizations and individual interests, embodying the purposes and spirit of the 1960 White House Conference, looks at children and youth nationally in broad perspective, focusing attention on the complex problems of children and youth in America. It is the only organization which embodies total concern, including social welfare, health, human growth and development, home and family life, education, agriculture, labor, housing, intergroup relations, religion and myriad other associated concerns.

The National Committee for Children and Youth provides a continuing constructive force at the national level to keep alive the energy and ideals of the White House Conference. It serves as a rallying point for the network of organizations, agencies and individuals united by a common love and concern for children. It maintains a continuous study of the needs of children and youth in our changing times. It identifies problem areas and focuses attention on the key issues emerging out of changing conditions. It promotes concerted action, provides consultative service and maintains a clearinghouse of information.

The Joy of Children is thus one way by which the National Committee carries out the goals of the White House Conference. More important, it may be a means of enhancing for many Americans their joy in children and of intensifying their intelligent devotion to them.

The Committee is proud indeed that Pearl Buck has provided the text for *The Joy of Children* and that she has written it with such heart. As a 1932 Pulitzer Prize winner and recipient of the 1938 Nobel Award in literature, Pearl Buck stands high in the ranks of American writers. And now, in *The Joy of Children*, her sensitivity to the universal and spiritual meaning of childhood adds another dimension to photography. The beauty and rhythm of her words combined with the appeal and vividness of the pictures has transformed an exhibit called, "These Are Our Children" into a book titled *The Joy of Children*.

This book, and the National Committee for Children and Youth, both offspring of the 1960 White House Conference, are dedicated to children and to those who love them.

Roy Sorenson, Chairman
National Committee for Children and Youth

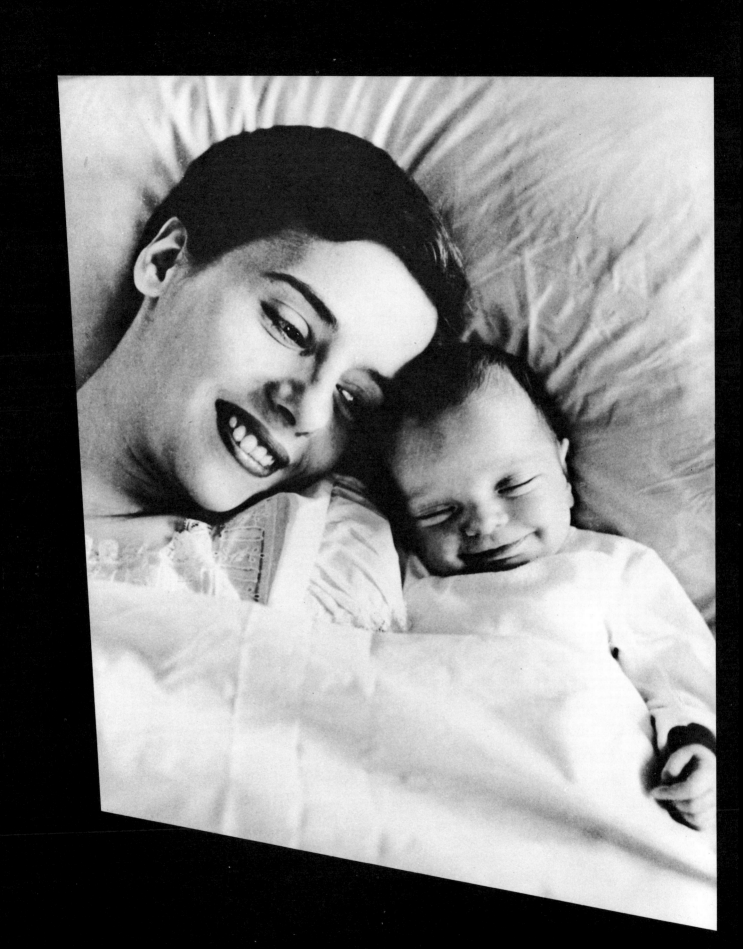

THE JOY OF CHILDREN

It is a joy which holds the world together, the joy of children. Children are world treasures. However far I travel, into the uttermost parts of the earth, I find the same love of children that enriches our own life here in the United States. Indian mothers and fathers in a remote village in Rajasthan love their children in the same way that American parents love their own. It is a love necessary to the fulfillment of life. The individual human cycle is not whole until man and woman look back to the parents who gave them life and forward to the children to whom they themselves give life. Only thus does the individual feel assured of his place in the eternal scheme of creation. Only thus does his heart find rest.

It is more than mere instinct, this love of children. It is a renewal of hope and faith. Who can gaze at a newborn baby and not wonder again at The Miracle? For it is the miracle, this emergence of a unified being, a separate creature, from fusion of two. Who can explain it? Who can explain the mysterious individual spirit living in this tiny new baby? No one knows what this spirit is or how it will grow or what it will become. The potential in any child is infinite. Yet it is a malleable infinity. It can be shaped, dwarfed, or developed by the genes in its history and by the circumstances of its experience. In the knowledge of such responsibility we tremble, we are awed, we are stirred to self-examination. Are we worthy of assuming power over these children? Dare we believe that we know good and evil well enough to teach them the difference? Do we ourselves know the difference, and do we choose the good in preference to the evil, or are we hypocrites, and if we are, how can we teach these innocent?

And looking at the faces of the children, whatever their race and kind, we see the same look, so touching in its gayety, its wonder, its trustfulness and readiness to love. A child is born with the readiness to trust and to love. Trust comes first, trust that someone will feed and tend a helpless creature, trust that sorrows will be comforted and pain assuaged. How sad the day, the hour, when that trust is betrayed! Yet children are incredibly forgiving. They continue to love when all reason for love is gone. Children will love their parents long after the parents may have proved themselves unworthy. It is very difficult to kill love in a child's heart but it can be done — yes, it can be done. And when it is done, when the child knows he is betrayed by one he loves and who should love him, the wound can never be mended. The child lives the rest of his life, however long, a wounded creature, unable ever again to love with trust. Call it what it is, a maimed life, and the most evil person in the world is he who so maims a child that he carries forever such a wound. It is easy to see from a child's face, from the look in his eyes, whether he has received the mortal wound.

I am not pleading for a soft, sentimental love of children. Indeed, children are the first to recognize the dangers in such love and sooner or later instinctively they will try to escape from it. For nothing repels a child more than sentimental selfish love, demanding a similar response. A healthy child knows that he must escape in order to grow, and he knows above all else that growth is essential if he is to live. Yet he seeks love and he must have it, for love is essential, too, to growth. But it must be an unselfish love, demanding no response except in the child's own growth. And is that not response enough? I know of no joy in life greater than the joy of seeing a child grow in mind and spirit and body, the small self-absorbed creature newly born, changing into the responsible, eager, active human being. This is the contented child, the happy child, feeling himself free and yet knowing the wisdom of a firm and just discipline, one which teaches self-discipline. And self-discipline is the goal, for without it there can be no achievement, and without achievement there is no permanent joy in life. To know the reach of one's abilities, to strive and to achieve that reach, this is happiness.

I see the children's faces in every part of the world, in every land and nation, and each face tells the child's story. Study the faces and know whether the child is loved and encouraged or unloved and without courage. A child has no subterfuge. A child hides nothing. He tells everything by the way he looks, by the way he behaves. A bevy of happy faces, you'd say? Not so fast, please! Study each face, separate from the crowd, and see which is the happy child and which is not.

Happy or not, children are our national treasure. With what measure we mete to them in their childhood, they will mete to our nation in their lifetime. Our investment of love, wise understanding guiding love, is the best investment we can make for the future, for children are our future. When I look at a child's hands, when I take a child's hands, so soft and seeming helpless, into mine, I see those same hands as they will be tomorrow, strong, competent, helpful, or weak and fumbling. Hands tell the story as well as faces do, but they tell it later, and they tell it with glorious courage or in distressful failure. They tell it in action, for better or worse.

The strength or weakness of a nation is in the hands of its children. Yet our children are what we make them. They come to us helpless, malleable, dependent upon what we provide. They leave us as men and women, the next generation, the blessed or the doomed.

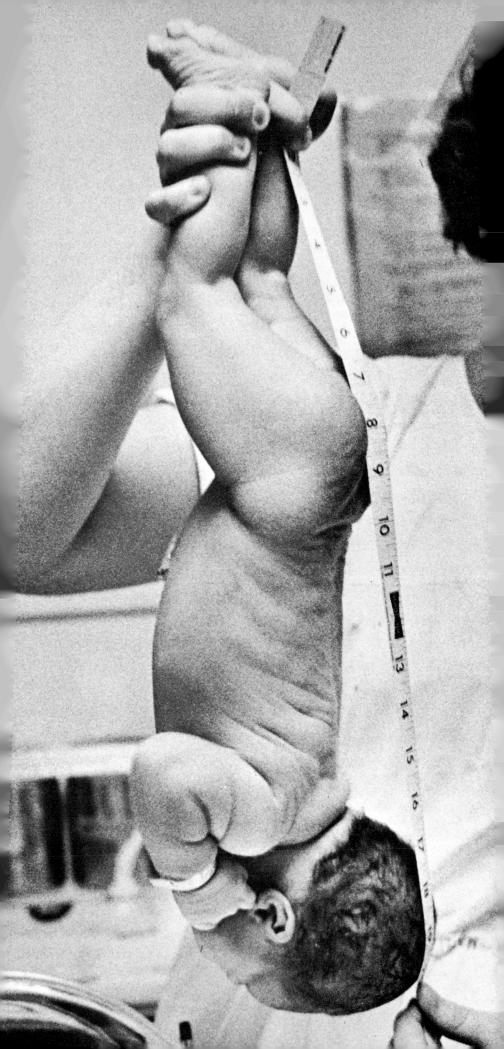

FOR ALL CHILDREN—WELCOME!

The first welcome is and must be from the mother. Long before the baby is born, even before he is conceived, the welcome begins. A little girl is developing that welcome when she plays with her doll. A young girl feels the welcome stirring in her heart when she responds to the first kiss from a boy. A woman in love, a woman who becomes a wife, knows her whole being is shaping to welcome the coming of a child. When the child is conceived all the warmth of the growing years comes to focus upon the small creature rising to life within her. She lives with the child most intimately for nine months and waits, impatient to welcome the birth.

This is the normal pattern of a woman's life, but pity the mother who dares not welcome her child! There are many such mothers. We call them the mothers of "illegitimate" children, as though any child could be born outside the laws of nature! Yet thousands of young girls give birth each year to children they do not welcome and thousands of women, loving men they cannot marry, hide these children in secret fear of discovery. Such children can find welcome only in an adoptive family, but most of them spend their lives as orphans. Our laws give protection to neither mother nor child when the child is born out of wedlock. There is a discrepancy here between law and fact. Extreme sexual freedom and sexual stimulation in our society result in the birth of the child for whom no welcome is waiting.

Yet the child, arriving according to the laws of creation, deserves welcome and can thrive only when he is welcome. Nor is it only the child who suffers when he is not welcome. The mother, not daring to welcome the child whom society does not welcome, feels her natural urge toward motherhood stopped and thwarted. It is an experience from which she never wholly recovers. Happy the mother who rejoices in the birth of her child, for this child brings joy into the world, joy to his parents, his family, his community. He starts life with an advantage more valuable than wealth and greater than royal blood.

Yet a welcome from his fellow human beings is the birthright of every child. How shall we guarantee him his birthright? It is not only the mother who must welcome him wholeheartedly. The father, too, must recognize his offspring and through such recognition accept the responsibilities of his part in creating a new human being. The child needs welcome from his father as well as his mother, and beyond them the community represented by the State, which registers and records his name and date of his arrival, and by the church, or synagogue, which welcomes him with special rites.

Of such recognition he is unaware while he is a baby. Food when he is hungry, the presence of his playful and adoring mother, the admiration of the public—ah, whose heart does not melt at the sight of the little newborn creature and what hidden memories and instincts are stirred! Did we all begin once upon a time, so small, so innocent, so tenderly cared for? Incredible in this hard, work-a-day world that once we were loved like that, and yet that today we are able so to love others is proof that once we were such small creatures, so tenderly cared for.

Yet babies have their sorrows. The bottle delayed opens up a hideous vista of hunger. The incomprehensible business of bathing and being weighed, the monstrous injustice of looking at the world from the bars of a pen or the rim of a gigantic modern planter, the shock of the grimacing face of a brother, the lovely luxury of lying in splendor, naked upon a leopard skin, these are only part of the extraordinary adventures of life. A baby learns more in the first year of his life than he ever learns again in any single year. A bold beginning, let us say, but not to be feared if he makes it in a circle of welcoming love.

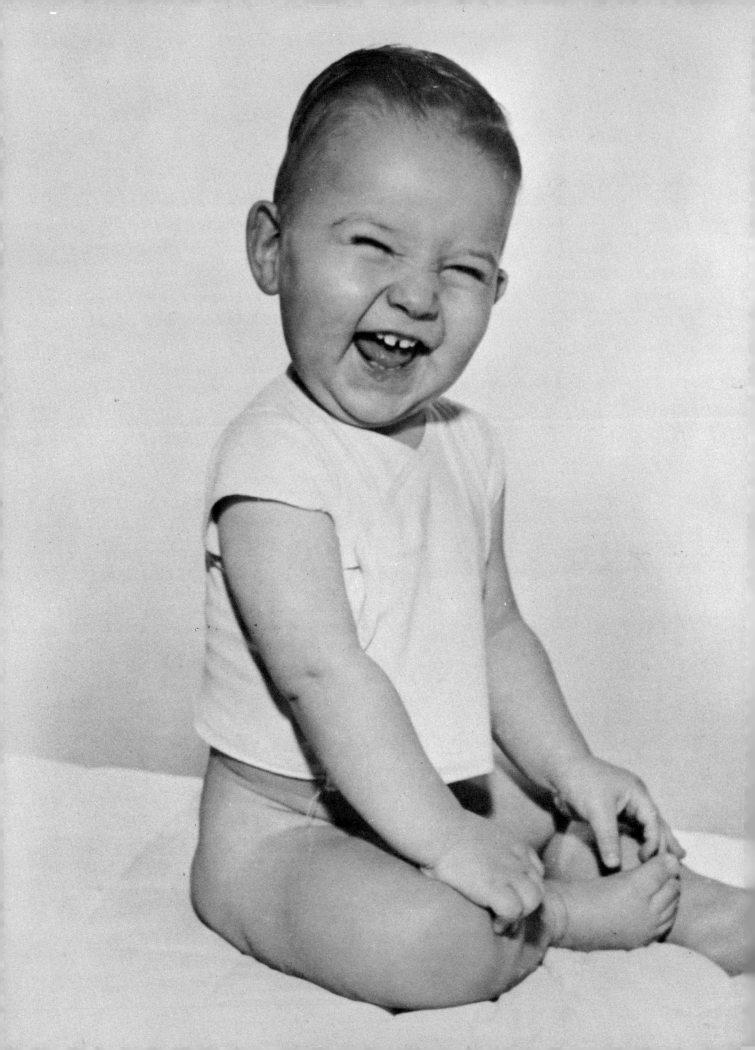

Welcome . . .

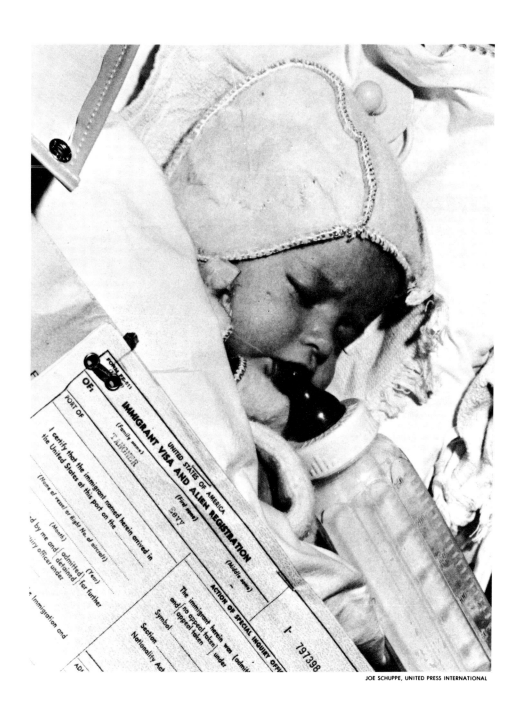

JOE SCHUPPE, UNITED PRESS INTERNATIONAL

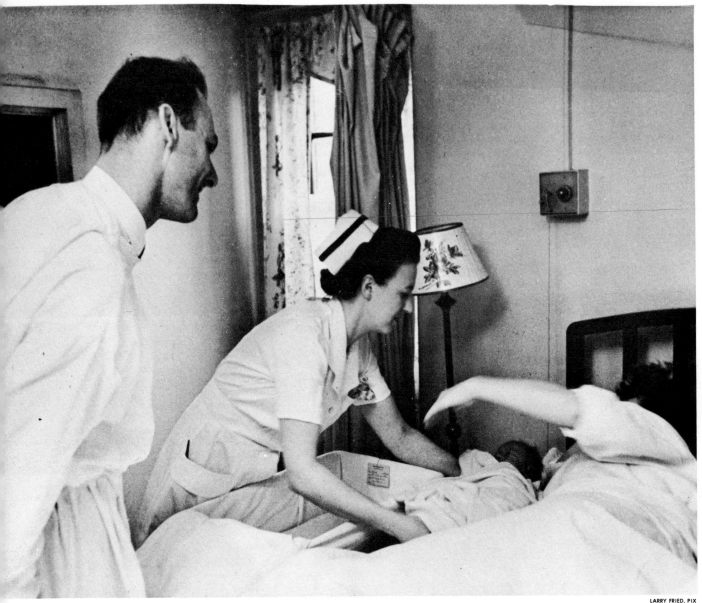

6

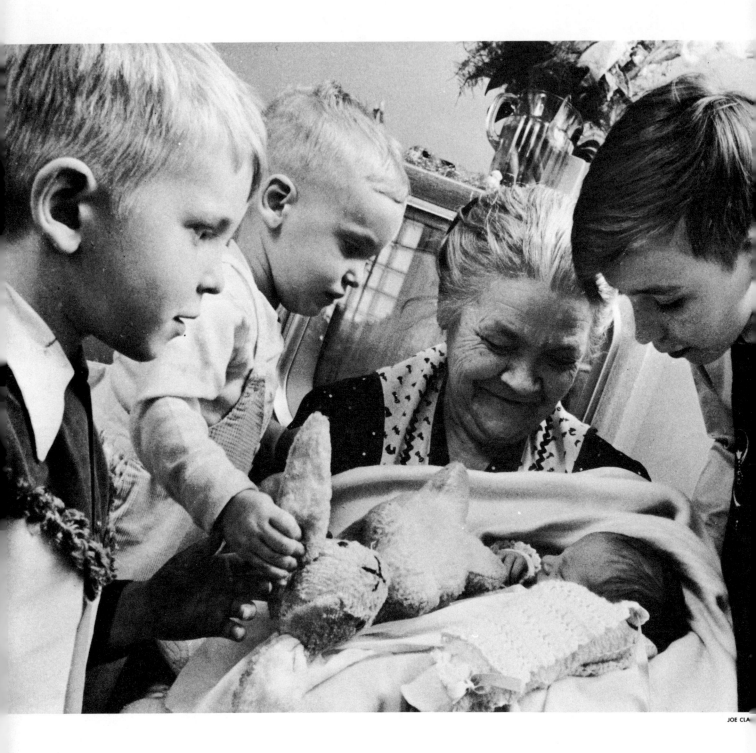

8

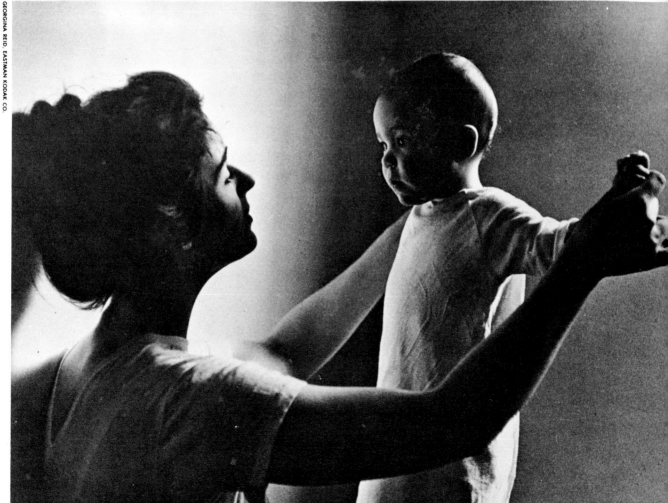

injustice . . . .

JOHN REES, BLACK STAR PUBLISHING CO.

LOOK MAGAZINE PHOTO

11

FOR EVERY CHILD — PROTECTION AND CARE; SECURITY AND LOVE

It is not enough to welcome a child into the world. He needs an environment of continuing love and security. The initial welcome must expand into an atmosphere in which he can grow and develop in every phase of his being, and with joy. Food, for example, is a necessity, good simple food, rich in proteins and vitamins, suited to his age and individual taste. It is important that he eats with enjoyment. This means that he must not be forced to eat, or hurried or scolded. Eating is a primary function of life. It should never be associated with anger or impatience. Manners should only come in due course. They are easily learned, but later, after one is well established in the principle that eating is fun. The enjoyment of food is psychologically related to the creation of a happy well-balanced habit of mind and body. Discipline and eating should not be carried on at the same time. Eating is so basic a function that a child should never connect it with the insecurity of being disapproved.

Security is based, of course, on the conviction that one is loved, or at least liked. Mother-love can be taken for granted. It serves its best for cuts and bruises and falls on slippery floors. Mother-love is sheltering arms, but what about father-love? It is as necessary, too, for a child's growth. The father is away all day, perhaps. Well, then, he must make all the more effort to find opportunity to express his love for his children. Without him they will grow warped. The mother can never compensate for the father, and the best way he can show his love is never to fail his child. Absolute truth in his dealings with the child, his word always kept when given, or if a promise must be broken, then full and early explanation, the building of a confidence so complete that the child can trust his father with his whole heart — this is the foundation of a child's security and indeed of his own integrity. For every child admires his father and wants to find him worthy of love. When he finds him not to be trusted, it is a shock from which the child never recovers. He never is able to trust anyone fully again, perhaps as long as he lives. And who can tell how strong a force his child's trust is, in the man's own life?

So reared, the child is ready to trust other people, too — doctors, for example, and nurses and teachers. These, too, are persons whom he must learn to trust. It is essential that children learn the necessity of regular dental care, of going to a doctor when they are ill, of following the advice of community health officers. Dentists and doctors are friends in need and health officers help us not only as individuals but as citizens living in a community, where all are mutually responsible for the common welfare.

The community is the family enlarged. The individual has his duty to perform in this larger family. The community, in return, has a responsibility for the individual. Its duty is to provide a healthy, encouraging, secure environment for every citizen. This really means every citizen, the intelligent, the normal, but also the weak, the handicapped. The good community, like the good parent, is aware not only of the physical needs of the child, but also aware and watchful of his emotional and psychological development.

One can judge a family's life by the way the children behave outside, the way they meet strangers, the self-discipline they show in a dentist's chair, on a surgeon's table, in the demands of community life. If they are secure at home, if they trust their parents and believe what they have been told in preparation, they meet crises with confidence in themselves and in others. See the little boy watching the hypodermic plunged into his arm! Certainly he does not enjoy the sight, but he understands why it is being done and he is able to control himself and cooperate.

It is pleasant to be liked, too, by persons outside the family group. A teacher's friendly gesture, a doctor's explanations, even a stranger's smile, add to the day's joy. What the child does not realize is that he wins this liking by being himself outgoing and friendly. He attracts by being attractive. And he is attractive because he is secure, first of all, at home and then in his community. He has all he needs. Rich or poor, he has food and decent clothes and something to call his own. Above all, he has friends. He knows he is loved and understood — and safe.

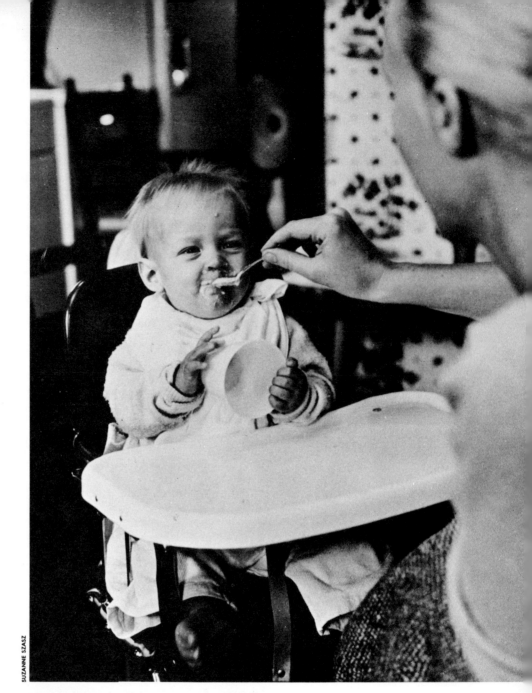

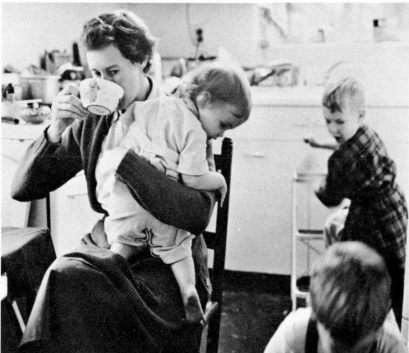

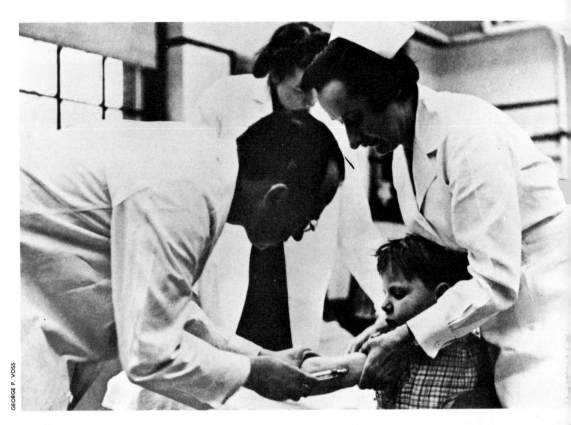

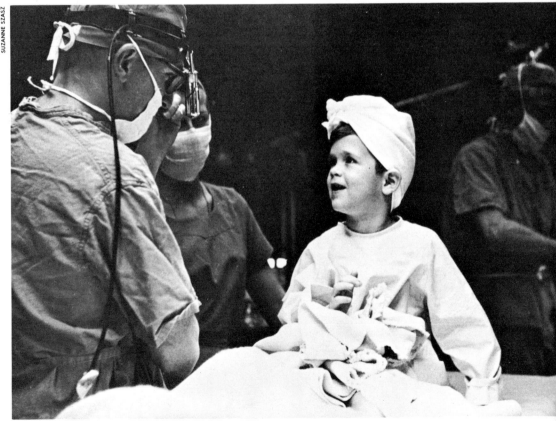

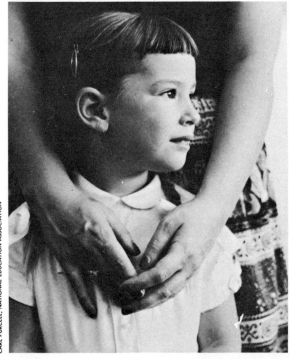

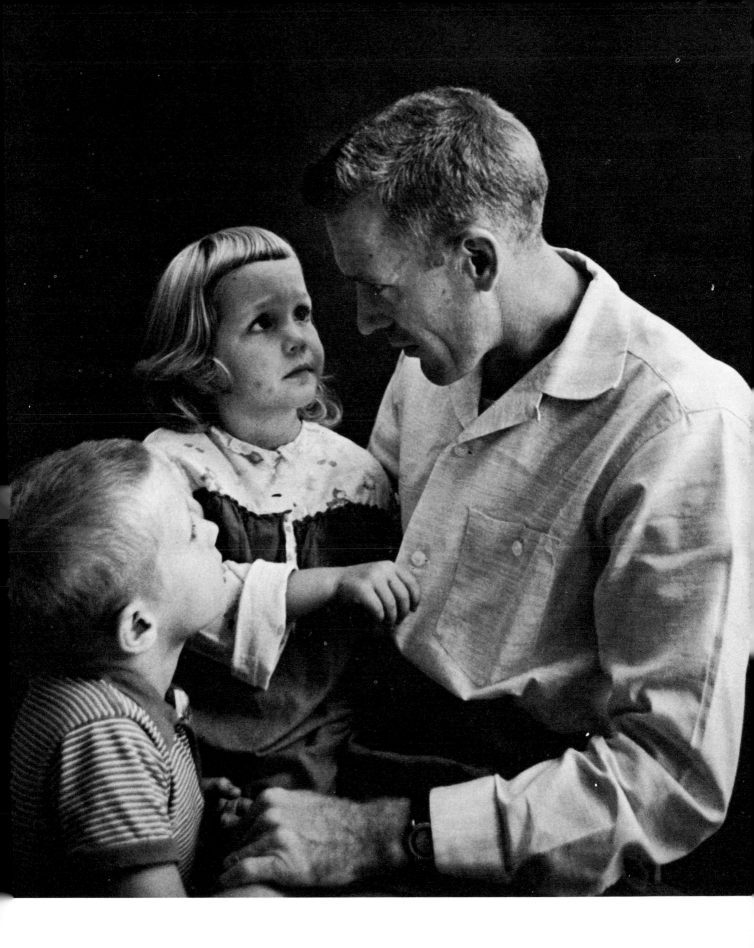

CHILDHOOD IS A TIME FOR DISCOVERY AND GREAT ADVENTURE

To thwart the desire of a child to explore his world is a dangerous suppression, affecting his entire mental outlook. Let us be proud of ourselves when our children say goodby gaily for they will certainly come back to tell us about their adventures, confident that we will be there to welcome them and ready to listen. How light the burden of loneliness when we know their confidence in us! Encourage adventure, all parents! Childhood is the time for discovery and adventure. It is nature's way of accommodating the expanding intelligence and the growing spirit.

"You want to know?" Nature inquires. "Then go and find out for yourself."

Let parents echo the command and let teachers repeat it in school. To cry a fear is to inject an emotion that may choke the growing spirit. Of course the cat may scratch the baby creeping toward it on all fours. There is doubt in the baby's eyes and in the cat's sidewise stare. They are making mutual inquiry. Let them make mutual answer. If the cat scratches, the baby will remember claws and cope with his own knowledge more easily than with his mother's fears. And face to face with a fawn, a little girl is overcome with the comedy of a goat's face, a natural comedy communicated without words, and a little boy sees how wide the world is from the vantage point of a stone wall on a mountain road, and learns how a machine obeys the man who knows how to use it, and a baby dares to face a family of white geese who stand as high as he does, nearly, provided he clutches his mother's skirt with one hand securely. Sand on a beach is another world upon which one leaves footprints, and television is a projection of one's own world and a barn is a dark cave into the unknown, and a pond is a place for mud and frogs, fish and reflections, and food comes from supermarkets and a birthday cake is a joy that comes only once a year, itself a symbol of growing. Water is a world for fishes, and ballet is hard work because body must obey mind, and mind has to learn how to discipline itself and body, too, and a little girl feels like a lady when she dresses up in lady's clothes — and a little boy has to learn how to behave like a man when he sits in the barber's chair.

A child grows through wonder and curiosity and adventure and new experiences with nature, animals and human beings. It is the duty and privilege of all adults, family and friends and teachers, to encourage this expansion of life, physical, mental and spiritual. If the child is secure in his home and community, especially if he knows he need not be afraid to leave home because it will be there when he comes home, waiting and welcoming, then he will face new life without fear.

SUZANNE SZASZ

MEYER LIEBOWITZ

DENNIS HALLINAN

PHOEBE DUNN

31

RUSSELL T. FORTE

33

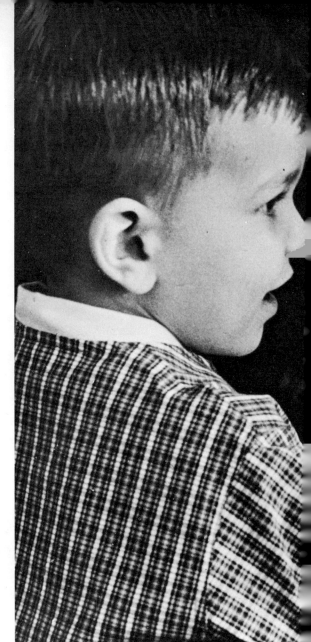

36

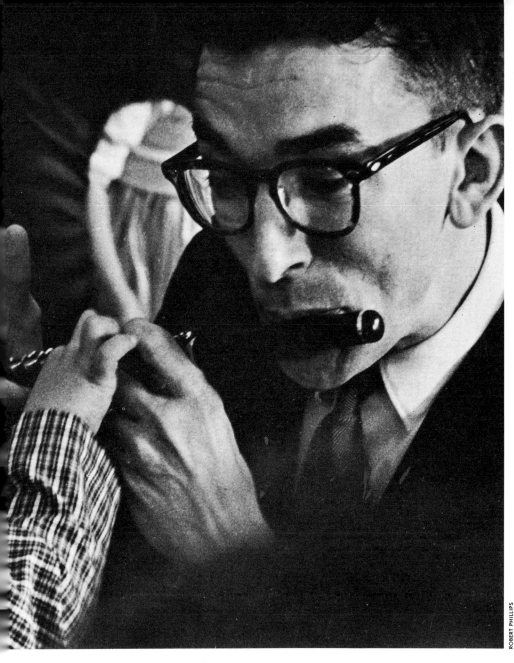

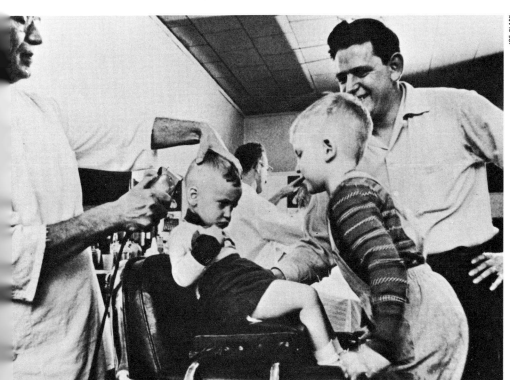

37

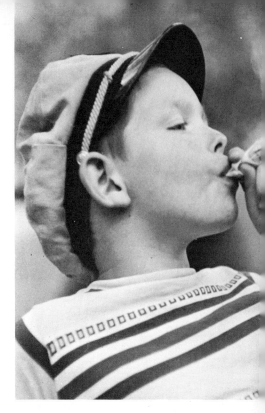

40

42

43

CHILDREN ARE PERSONALITIES IN THEIR OWN RIGHT

When a child is able to seek and find adventure and new experience, when he can shake hands with President Eisenhower, for example, and conduct himself with suitable aplomb, when he can go alone to a baseball game, or even manage a lively horse with enjoyment, it is time for all persons to recognize him as an individual human being and treat him accordingly. When a little girl can visit a museum and respond to what she sees there with unconscious abandon, then she has something of her own free spirit to communicate. The truth is that the child is an individual from the moment he — or she — is born, and should have been so treated from the first appearance upon the stage called life. Let us not, as parents, allow ourselves the conceit of saying "This is my son," or "my daughter." Introduce the child to strangers by his own name as a person standing in his own right, and though connected with a family, the family is of secondary importance. It is as John or Mary that one functions as a responsible human being.

If the child has been treated from birth with respect certain qualities and habits develop. First of all, he respects himself as a person, not merely as the son of so-and-so, or the daughter, and this no matter how famous the so-and-so may be. With self-respect comes pride in one's behavior and deportment. Self-respect demands certain virtues, such as truth-telling, cleanliness and industry. Something is expected and pride in one's self, which is totally different from conceit, responds to expectation.

At the same time, satisfaction with one's self removes inhibitions. One need not pretend with other people, when one is self-confident. One can be frankly gay, for example, while eating a hamburger and wearing a cock-eyed hat, or putting on an apron and puttering in the kitchen sink, or prancing up and down the aisle in a plane or train or hiding behind a tree or inviting the cat to play, or wearing a pair of grown-up goggles or even sticking out one's tongue. In short, self-confidence provides another kind of security, a further development toward the total security which makes a person dare to live and with joy.

In a big family, of course, each child must be given individual respect and a consideration framed upon his being. Even twins should be considered separately and alone. And a child's moods should not be lightly ignored. No one lives in a state of euphoria or should so live. When a child too big to suck his thumb crouches beside a rocking chair, thumb in mouth, he has received a wound within. As a human being he deserves consideration. Pity is all wrong, and sympathy may not be wise. What he needs is intelligent concern. He may need someone to lead him to understand himself through self-revelation. A quiet, calm and friendly approach is the means. A tear in the eye of a little girl, a finger in the mouth, constitute a need. There is a break in self-respect.

The Chinese have a beautiful word for it. The face changes, they say, loses its joys, the lines droop, when the self receives a shock. "Diu lien," they call it, or "face-drooping." One must do nothing to bring about this change, they say, for expression of the face is the outward manifestation of the inner being. "Lose face," is the way we have sometimes translated the Chinese phrase into English — a wrong translation of words which declare with delicate precision that self-respect must never be destroyed by carelessness or cruelty, lest the inner being suffer irremediable damage.

47

51

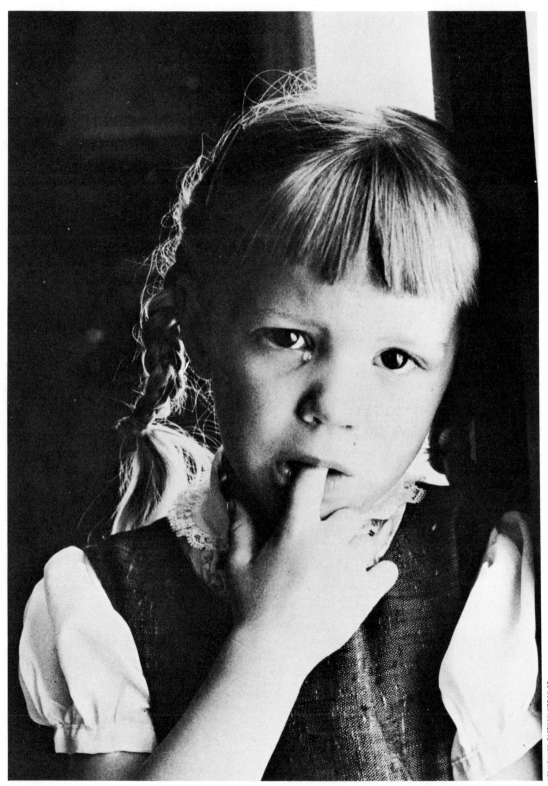

54

THEY NEED A WHOLESOME
SETTING FOR FAMILY LIFE

Let me give as an axiom the fact that all children must have a secure home life if they are to develop into good and loving adults, happy to be alive. A secure home life is to be found first of all in good and loving parents. Second, it is to be found in a pleasant living place, whatever its limitations. Of these two basic requirements I fear the first is most often lacking in American life today. There are reasons for this. The rash of too young marriages which set in at the end of World War II and which still continues, has produced too young parents, themselves boys and girls, too immature to know what true love is. They have not outgrown the selfishness of adolescence, and they are selfish in marriage and as parents.

Now selfishness in adolescence is normal and to be expected. It may even be necessary, as the young human being struggles toward independence, it is inevitable that he centers temporarily on himself. But there should be no selfishness in love, if marriage is to be a success, and certainly parents cannot be selfish toward their children and have happy and normal children. Yet how often one sees too young mothers more interested in their own clothes and appearance than in how their children look and how often one sees young husbands and fathers out with "the boys," rather than thinking of wife and children!

Our American family life is changing without one being aware of it and it is not only the too young marriages that are changing it. The change in American women since the end of World War II is more profound than we know, in spite of the many books being published on the subject. To put it concisely, it appears that the American woman in increasing numbers has decided, or is deciding to abandon the double standard and is accepting for herself the freedom in sex habits heretofore traditional only for men. The result inevitably is an instability in marriage and consequently in home life. The ancient stigma of unchastity is fading. It never existed for men and may cease to exist for women in the foreseeable future. Only upon the child born out of wedlock does the burden still fall. He is born without a home and without parents. Of the more than 200,000 children born out of wedlock each year in the United States more than half find no adoptive homes. Even adoption does not wholly fulfill their need. The cruelty of other children and in some measure of society condemns them. "Your real mother was a whore," is an insult all too commonly flung at the adopted child by his schoolmates. His disturbance is often severe and one is led to question whether it should not now be considered that a new sort of family should be recognized, one where the mother and her child or children constitute a unit. It is not ideal, for the child needs both parents, but at present he is deprived of both and is without status.

Children need a healthful setting for life, and the first essential is stability, both in human relationships and physical environment. Of the two I put human relationships first. A child can stand an amazing amount of change in environment if his family remains constant. There are families in Asia who never have a home or land, whose home is a city pavement, their shelter in storm a gateway, and yet whose children grow up with surprising emotional equilibrium because they are always with their parents. It is not normal for children to be alone. They have to know where their parents are, how to reach them in case of need, and be able to rely on their return at the appointed time.

Yet a child's healthful setting is more than a house or rooms to live in. The house, the rooms, must be coordinated and created into a home, a place where parents and children together can carry on the activities of life in an atmosphere encouraging and creative. It is at home with the busy but loving mother that children learn the necessity and pleasure of good, well-cooked food. It is at home that children learn the joy of sharing holiday excitement, or the tranquil everyday pastimes of reading and play.

Play is a child's real life. There must be time and space for play, solitary play when the mind can create in fruitful loneliness and play, too, in which the whole family shares. Outdoor play is essential, adventures by sea and land. A child needs to live in a wide world.

Yet many a child lives in a world no wider than a hovel, in a city slum. We are beginning to realize that slums produce warped human beings. We are clearing away the slums. Every time a ramshackle building on a crowded street is torn down and replaced by a clean modern building the result can be measured in children growing up with healthy men and women.

I add only one word of caution. If the rents are too high, both parents may feel they must work outside the home. When this happens, it is possible that the best of housing provides no home. A house is only a house, palace or slum, if a child comes home to no one. The problem of the working mother is still unsolved. Sometimes she is compelled to work because the father cannot earn enough to support the family. Sometimes she works to relieve her own restlessness. Whatever the reason, the problem is for the parents to solve — only never let it be at the expense of the child whom they have brought into life.

SUZANNE SZASZ

ST. LOUIS POST DISPATCH, BLACK STAR PUBLISHING CO.

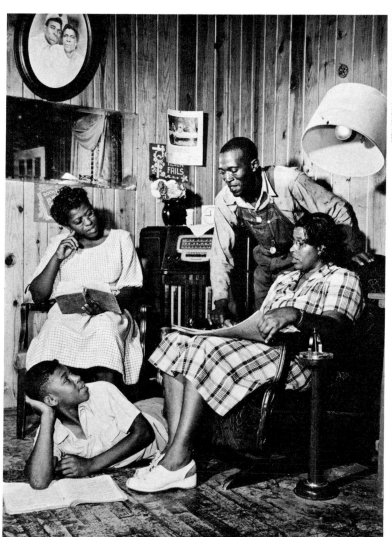

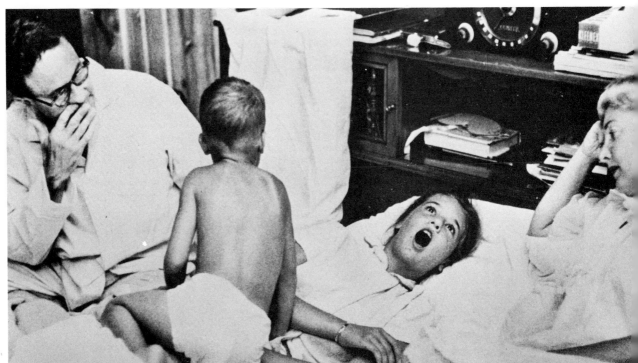

LOOK MAGAZINE PHOTO

ED BURKE, BLACK STAR PUBLISHING CO.

71

73

A PLACE TO PLAY CAN BE THE BEST PART OF GROWING UP

For adults the most satisfying hours of life are those spent in interesting and absorbing exciting work. What such work provides for adults is provided for children in interesting, absorbing, exciting play. For what is interesting is absorbing, and what is absorbing is exciting, since these qualities demand the utmost of a person's capacity to perform, to achieve and to enjoy. Nothing in life is more finally satisfying than this enjoyment of achievement and performance. These are the lasting values, the desires for work, the capacity to be absorbed in work, and the enjoyment of success in work. In such activity the self is fulfilled, individually and in relationship to others. Thus the child discovers first in play the lasting values of his entire life.

How is the discovery made? It must be made in freedom. His world is his playground. Special places are welcome enough, swings and climbing poles, swimming pools and baseball fields are places for teamwork and the discipline of shared goals and the rules of the game. But there must be too the wilderness of sea and forest, a low hung tree where children can play at being monkeys. If there is a barn where animals live, so much the better, for they teach children responsibility and compassion, and they teach the simple story of life and its creation.

Wherever children are, play must be, for they will make it, since through play they learn the lessons of life. Blessed are the children who live in peaceful places, in space and beauty, blessed are they when they can play under the loving eyes of family, in pleasant communities and among friends, but if these are lacking, they will play on ash cans and in dingy basements, in the streets of slums or pursuing a hockey puck among crowding cars, diving into rivers filthy with garbage, climbing into the empty windows of a ruined house, anywhere that children are, they play, imitating in play the life they see about them. Play is indeed the imitation of life, the effort of a child to take part in the accomplishment that his elders call work. It is creative activity, developing the mind and the imagination of the child. In that sense it is also the pursuit of happiness. In play the child finds satisfaction for his entire being, his body is strengthened, his mind refreshed and energized, his imagination inspired.

This is true, unfortunately, even when play, always modeled on what the child discovers in his environment, is destructive and antisocial. If the child believes the policeman is his enemy instead of his protector and friend, law becomes something to defy. Slums and extreme poverty, the wretched homes and ignorant, uncaring parents are the seed ground for play through which the child tries to reconcile himself to his misery by defiance and attack. Never to see the beauty of meadow and sea, never to know the discipline of organized games but only the wild law of the gang, can lead only to play which destroys. But the child plays on, compelled by his nature, to act out, in the only activity he knows, life as he sees it.

79

89

OUR CHILDREN LEARN TO DEVELOP LASTING VALUES

The instinct for beauty is native to the human heart and undying as long as life lasts. If I were asked what element is most important in a child's life, I would say the element of beauty. In beauty we find inspiration to create with joy; in beauty we find rest and consolation when sorrowful, and none can escape sorrow somewhere along the way. Yet children must be taught to discover beauty. They crave it, they accept it with ecstasy, but they cannot always create it or even find its whereabouts. They must learn to find it in art, in great paintings, in music and books, in landscape and sea and sky, in the noble human beings, living or dead, in the loyalties of friendship and family, in the love of country and of God. Through the perception of beauty the spirit grows strong in hope and courage. Without such perception the wings never spread, the mind lives in shadow, and the heart fails.

Shown what beauty is, however, the child pursues it, and in the pursuit he discovers his own talents and so himself. He tries many pathways of experience in home and community. In school, beyond his books, he tries music and dramatics and sports. In church he learns the beauty of worship and of the soul inspired. He learns, too, how to serve God and what the dedicated life means. In museums he sees the work of other dedicated men and women, those who devote their lives to creating beauty through art. In the presence of the great dead, at the feet of Abraham Lincoln, or gazing at the face of George Washington, he learns of dedication to the high demands of country and mankind. The flag becomes a precious symbol and he knows himself one of a great company called a nation. Through group play and congregation, he understands that he is not solitary. He is surrounded by many, a part of them and they of him. And when he learns to read, it is to come to know a greater host of men, women and children and to be identified with them. Above all, he learns the joy of learning. His world is infinitely enlarged, and ahead of him he sees the illumined path of more and more to know, as long as he lives.

ROBERT PHILLIPS

98

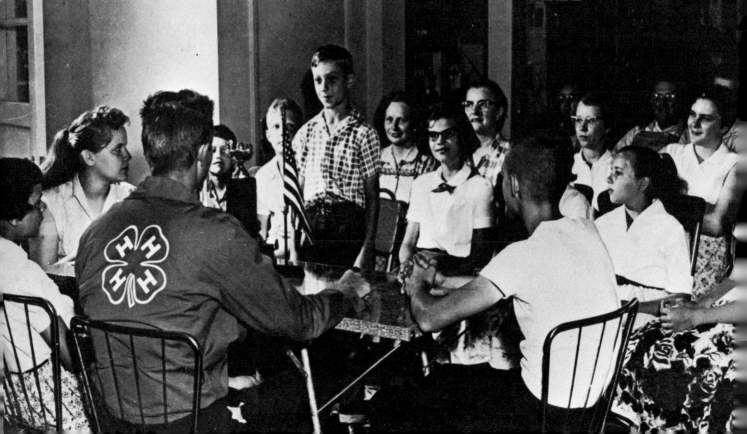

101

LOOK MAGAZINE PHOTO

NNENFELD

TOM E. WALTERS, PIX

103

106

OUR CHILDREN LEARN TO USE THEIR INDIVIDUAL ABILITIES

The child discovers not only the outer world of sense and object but he discovers, too, the inner world of self. What sort of person is he and what can he do? What gifts of genes and talents has he inherited from his ancestors?

What we are, what we can do, and how, these are the questions to be asked of self and answered through self-knowledge. But we can only know the self that is ours by knowing first many others. A wide experience of people, the realization that we are one of them, yet different, is the beginning.

And what should we do in life?

I always tell my own children, "Find out what you enjoy doing best of all and find a way to earn your living by doing it. Then you will never be bored or lonely.

You won't know the difference between work and play. It will all be fun."

To find joy in work is to discover the fountain of youth. Time never lags when work is keenest pleasure, labor is never to be dreaded. The secret of joy in work is contained in one word — excellence. To know how to do something well is to enjoy it. True, it takes effort to achieve that goal. The first drawing upon a piece of paper, how beautiful it looks in the mind and how disappointing it is when one sees it done. How glorious it is to sing in unison, but what if one sings out of tune? And how puzzling figures in arithmetic can be, how the mind rebels, yet what joy when the answer comes out clear and true! The discipline of the body is as difficult as the discipline of the mind, the wayward arms and legs, the awkward whole, that must learn how to obey the mind on the gymnasium floor or in the swimming pool, yet what release when effort brings success!

Confucius, five hundred years before Christ, declared that every child should learn the disciplines of music. I think he was right. Music creates harmony not only in sound but in the mind and body. Lips, voices, hands, must work in harmonious effort to create the music that the inner ear already hears. When this effort is successful, one knows the supreme joy of work well done.

The axiom is as true for the activities of modern life as it was for the ancient days of an old Chinese saga. To learn how to use a machine rightly is essential to our daily lives, providing sometimes the difference between life and death. Efficiency depends upon effort and joy in work depends upon efficiency. What is that joy? It is simply the satisfaction of knowing how a thing should be done and doing it that way. It is the satisfaction of rightness which we call excellence.

112

114

OUR CHILDREN LEARN TO PREPARE FOR THEIR FUTURE ROLE IN LIFE

Surely ours is the most exciting and significant age of all human history in which to live, and to be young in such an age is heaven. It is a new age, an age of fresh approach to old knowledge. Mathematics, for example, long embalmed, has suddenly come to life in terms of basic relationships, expressed in realistic symbols. So swiftly is new knowledge poured upon us from laboratories all over the world that our educational systems can scarcely keep up with all we are being told. Education today is a fluid process. What is considered a fact today may not be a fact tomorrow. It was once thought impossible, for example, that we could ever travel at the speed of sound. Now we take it for granted that we can break the sound barrier, and it is the speed of light that seems impossible. The one principle that holds true is that the changeless is changeable, the impossible is possible. This is the principle upon which all education today must be based, if we are to give our children the attitude toward life which will provide them with the outlook necessary for the expanding future.

Meanwhile the essential word is enthusiasm. It is an indictment of our school system today for any child to be bored in school. If boredom exists it is because the teacher is not trained for the new age, or the school is obsolete, or the members of the school board are too old and behind the times. It is a crime against the child if he is not enjoying the process of learning. It is a loss to the nation if he is not being properly prepared for the future through learning how to use his individual abilities and so fit himself for his role in life.

In school rooms and laboratories the process of education goes on, building the future of nation and world as it shapes the minds, spirits and bodies of our children. Yes, and their children, too, for these young people are the parents of the next generation. It will be a stronger, healthier, happier generation, for girls are learning how to make good homes and how to care for children. In classrooms, too, young men are learning how to be good men, good husbands, good fathers, "learning to do, doing to learn, earning to live, living to serve."

Above all, perhaps, girls and boys are learning how to work together in these classrooms, not in competition between male and female, but as individuals in a cooperative society, and with the same goals. Variety is the key word for both, the infinite variety of the fields of possible learning and therefore of achievement. The enlargement of scientific knowledge, the skills required in many fields, the opportunities for new kinds of work, all mean variety in life. This variety should not depress or frighten. Indeed it should excite and stimulate mind and imagination. We do indeed live in a new world. And, as always, it takes the effort of birth to adjust to what seems, but is not, sudden. The moment of physical birth, for example, must seem frighteningly sudden to the newborn child. He is expelled from the safe old world. He must do what he has never done before, he must draw a breath. Upon that instant of breathing life itself depends. If he fails to adjust to the new atmosphere, the unknown environment, he dies. He makes the effort and lives.

Yet birth is not sudden and the world itself is never new. Slow development precedes the birth and the world changes slowly. It is only the realization of change that seems sudden. To accept change and adjust to it in one's self is to grow. Variety and change — these are the normal aspects of our world.

EVE ARNOLD, MAGNUM PHOTOS, INC.

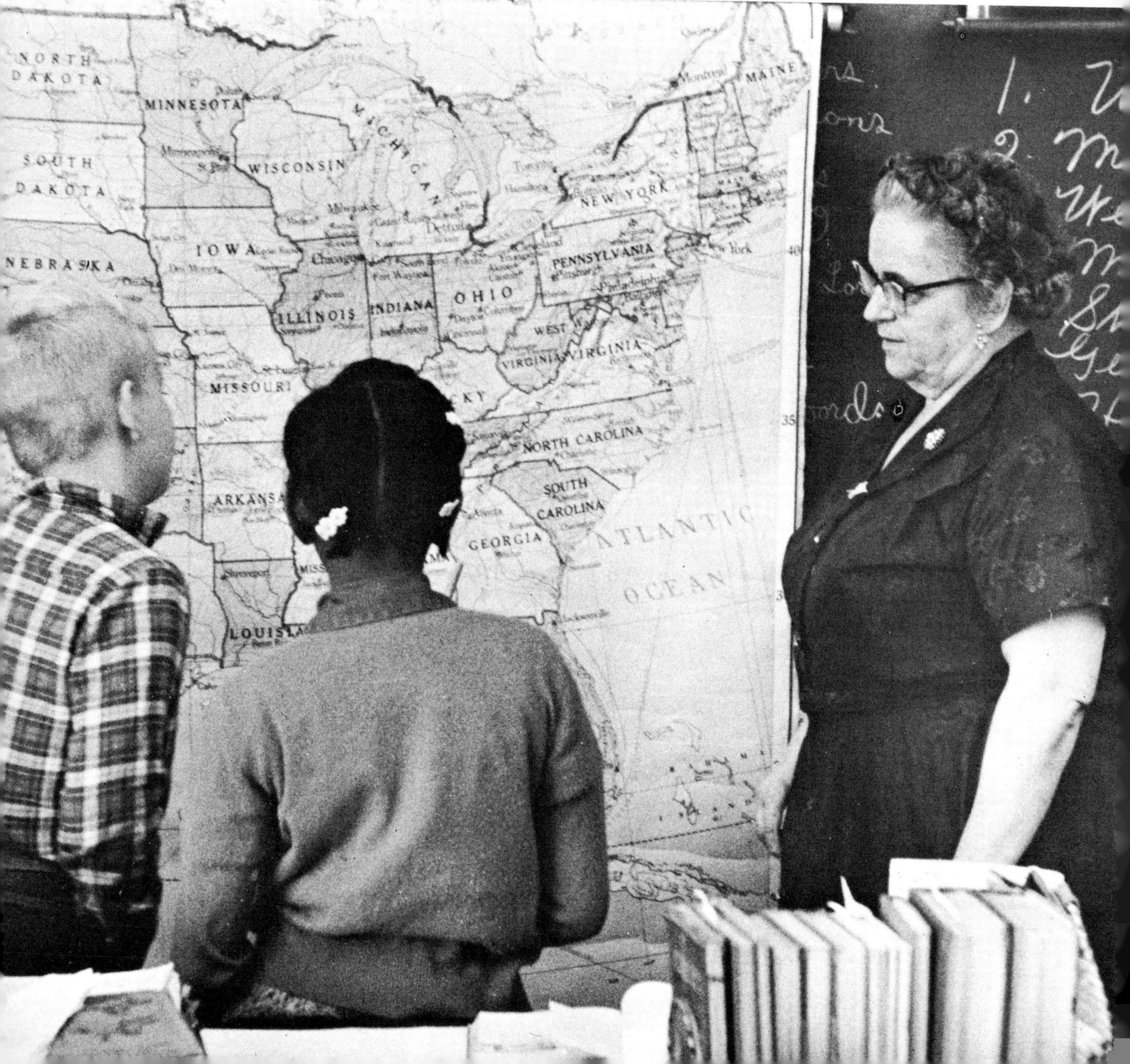

GEORGE TAMES

DENNIS STOCK, MAGNUM PHOTOS, INC.

122

ELLIOTT ERWITT, MAGNUM PHOTOS, INC.

124

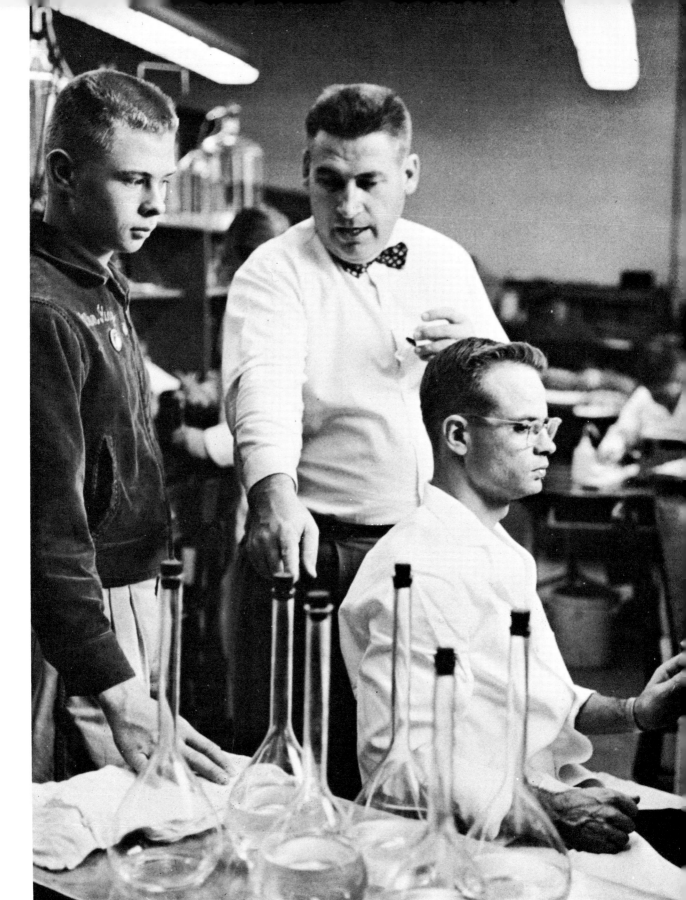

FRED MAROON

125

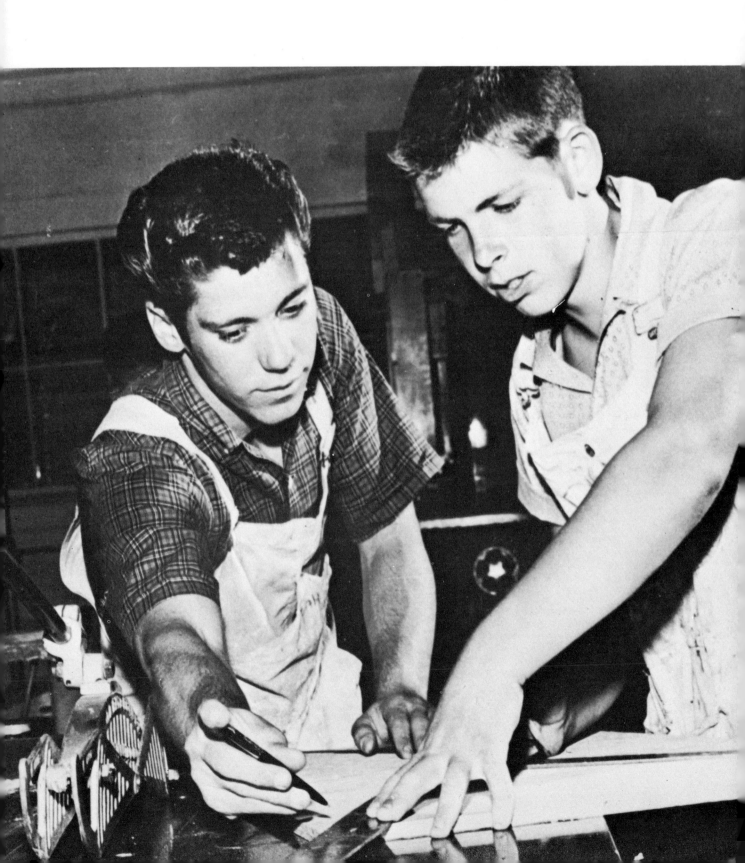

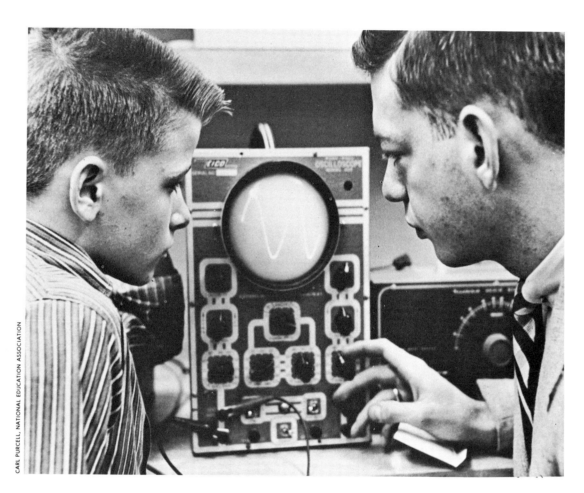

BERTRAND MILES

ED FEINGERSH, PIX, INC.

THE HANDICAPPED FIND HELP
AND CONFIDENCE

The handicapped child has the same rights that the more fortunate child has. In our Republic all citizens have the right to opportunity. This means the right to develop to the best of one's capacity. And development to some degree is always possible. The simplest mind can grow, the most broken body can struggle forward.

Sometimes, of course, a special atmosphere is necessary for growth. A slow mind becomes confused in the tensions of competition with normal minds. When a child cannot walk he must not be expected to run. We are beginning to understand that the handicapped children need special schools and specially trained teachers. Their families, distressed and bewildered, need help in understanding the handicapped child. The community must realize the handicapped citizen is part of the community, for inevitably a certain percentage of any human group is born with some defect, or is injured by war wounds or accident, and should not therefore be relegated or segregated. It is true that certain individuals must live within the protection of an institution, yet our overcrowded institutions contain many individuals who could live happily and usefully in their own homes if their communities would accept the fact that they are handicapped and provide for them the necessary training for livelihood geared to local job opportunities.

How many communities have in their public buildings, their churches and theaters, at least one entrance possible for someone in a wheelchair? How many industries review their activities to see which can be carried on by people with less than average mentality? Experience with the handicapped proves that when they are trained for certain routine jobs, they perform better than the more restless normal mind.

Yes, they deserve their place in the sun, these whom we call the handicapped. They must be brought out of the shadows. And how much they do for us, while we seek to do for them! They keep our hearts tender, these handicapped children. We discover that justice to them awakens us to justice everywhere. The quality of a civilization is measured in terms of what it does for these whom we call weak. It is essential for our own sakes that this quality be maintained. Let us remember that Hitler began his monstrous regime by killing the handicapped in institutions. Justice and mercy departed from the human spirit and before the end of the terror, twenty million people were dead in the most inhuman age of man's history on earth.

The handicapped child has much to teach us. The very recognition of his rightful place in the human family ennobles our spirits. When he is given the opportunity to grow he makes us humble as we watch his heroic efforts to improve himself, to achieve in spite of his handicap. And we learn about ourselves as we learn about him. Much that we have discovered in our efforts to help the handicapped has been of use to the normal human being, too, from the Binet tests brought to our country from France to test the mentally retarded now used to test all children, to the extraordinary facts we are discovering about metabolism and chromosomes in our recent research into the causes for mental retardation.

Yes, our handicapped children are valuable citizens, never to be forgotten for their sakes and ours, too.

And who has the most joy, the teacher who teaches a blind child how to read through his fingertips, or the blind child who discovers that the shapes under his finger tips are speaking to him in words that he can understand? Is there a greater delight in life than seeing the mind of a sightless child, a deaf child, begin to grow through communication? If there is, I do not know it. The light of understanding informs the whole being. The teachers of such children are different, too, from others. They are filled with the joy of overcoming difficulty, and helping the child to overcome.

The relationship between teacher and pupil in such case is like no other. It is more than teaching and learning. It is a communication of spirit with spirit, through minds and bodies. A physical therapist, helping a child to walk, does far more. The child is inspired through his teacher. He learns confidence in himself because he has confidence in his teacher. His sense of helplessness is replaced by a certainty that he can be independent at last. He works for that independence, drawing strength through his teacher's hope and faith. It is no wonder that these teachers walk with such an air of achievement and triumph.

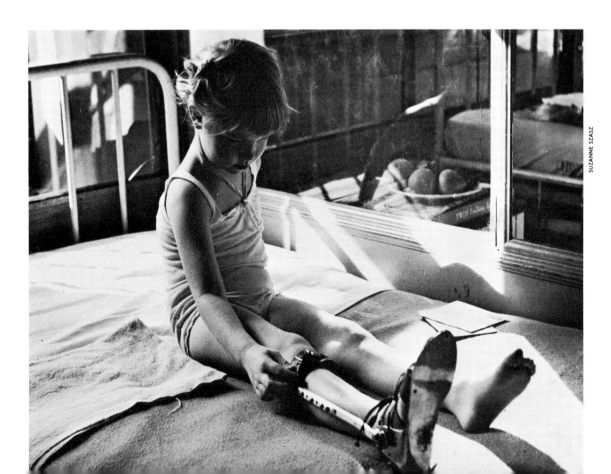

143

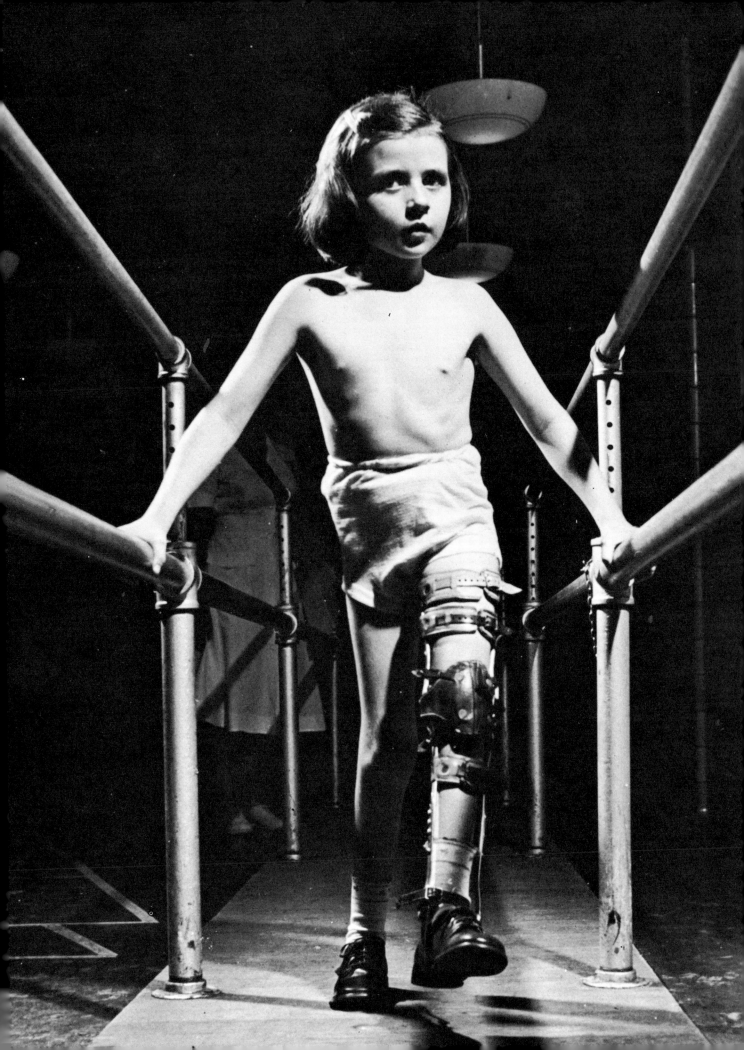

145

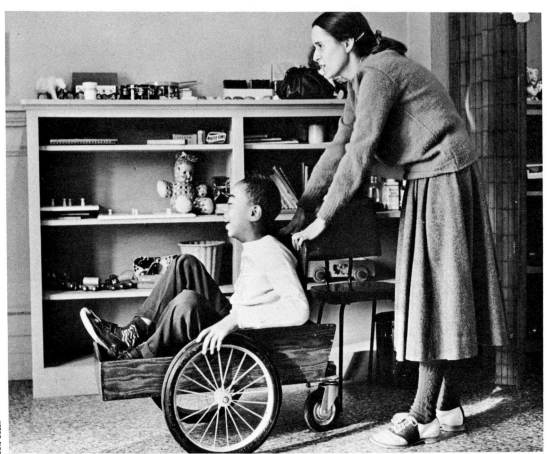

148

WIDE WORLD PHOTOS, INC.

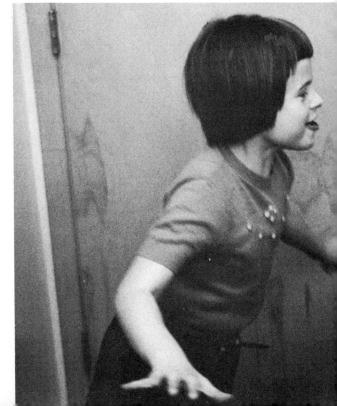

150

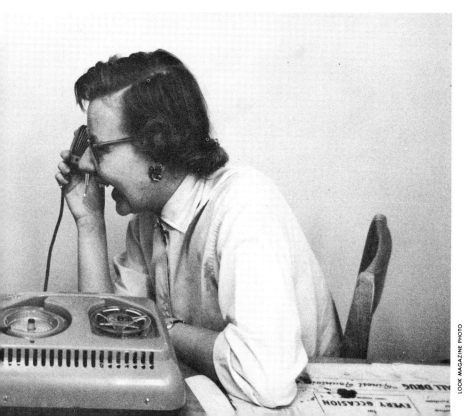

151

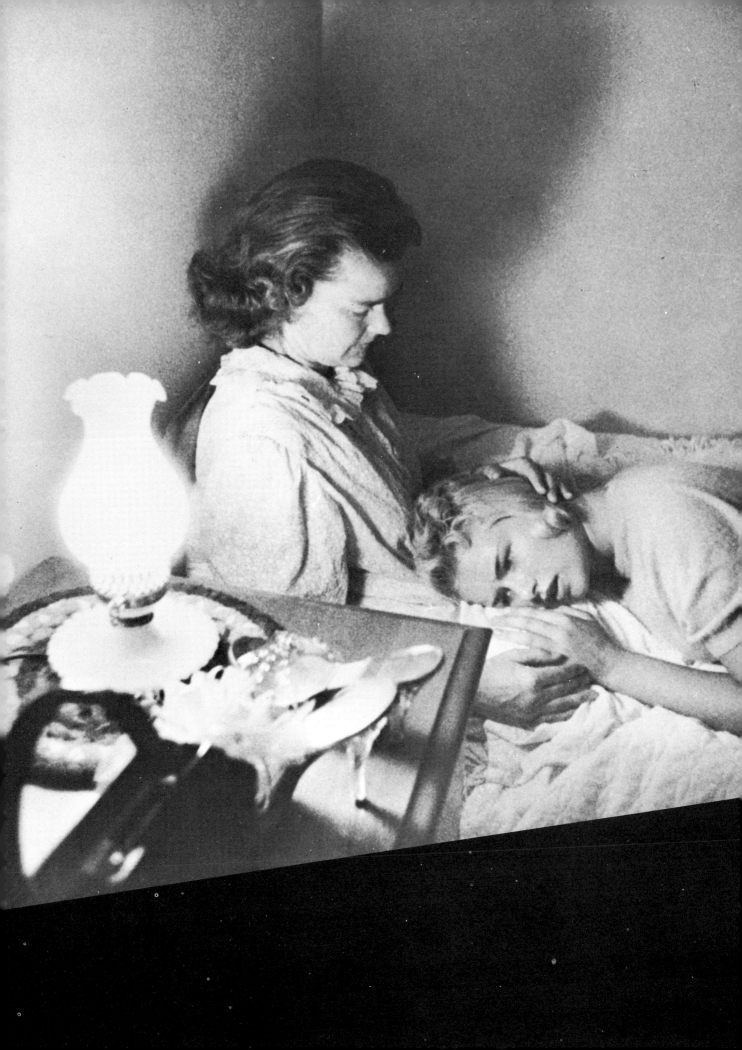

OFTEN, PATHWAYS TO MATURITY ARE NOT CLEAR

With all the help they have, it is not easy for our children to grow up in a competitive society. A home into which a child is born, the security of rooms he knows, his center of life, may be taken from him by the loss of a job. It leaves a scar on his memory. No house will ever be quite safe again unless someone in whom he believes tells him that there will be another home, perhaps one he will like even better. Sometimes it is a greater loss than a house. Sometimes it may be the loss of a father or mother through divorce or death. How can that loss be explained to the child whom they brought into the world? How can it ever be explained when an older sister is married and must leave home to build a new home of her own?

The peerage of something hard to bear comes when one goes to school the first day and he is left among strangers — teachers they may be but strangers for all of that, and the other children are strangers. What fearful loneliness in the midst of strangers! How can he believe that these strangers will ever be his friends? And when, as the days pass, the child learns that they are, what despair when a teacher whom one loves turns into a stranger again in a sudden temper, or the umpire decided unfavorably on the ballfield, or an admired scoutmaster seems suddenly stern and unfriendly because the "code" has been broken! The child has to learn that people change, with or without reason, he has to learn that friends can and do disagree and even resort sometimes to physical battle and yet afterwards be reconciled.

The hardest lessons of all to be learned are the lessons of growing up. The sadness of loving without return is just as hard at sixteen as it is at twenty-six, and the loneliness of adolescence can be the worst of all. A lad in the army far from home, a friendless young man in an empty street, a young man without a job and no one to help or care, a girl whose mother cannot understand, these are the sorrows that can lead to death of the spirit.

Fortunately they seldom so lead. Ours is a basically friendly society and there are those who exist to serve. A loving parent can help a girl to know at sixteen that all of life still lies ahead, waiting for her. An understanding priest or pastor or rabbi can help a boy to think his way through his problems.

Youth is the age of temptation and the greatest temptation of all is to do what the rest of the gang are doing, right or wrong. Too often it is wrong, for wisdom comes only with maturity, and the road to the maturity of self-understanding and self-discipline is long and hard and there are those who never reach the end of that road.

ROLAND PATTERSON

NOLAN PATTERSON II, BLACK STAR PUBLISHING CO.

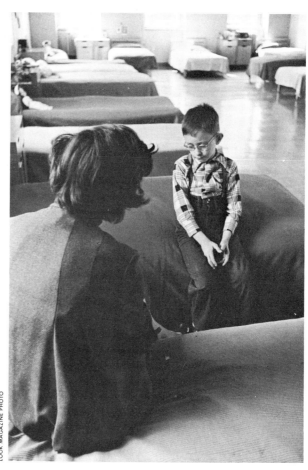

WAYNE MILLER, MAGNUM PHOTOS, INC.

LOOK MAGAZINE PHOTO

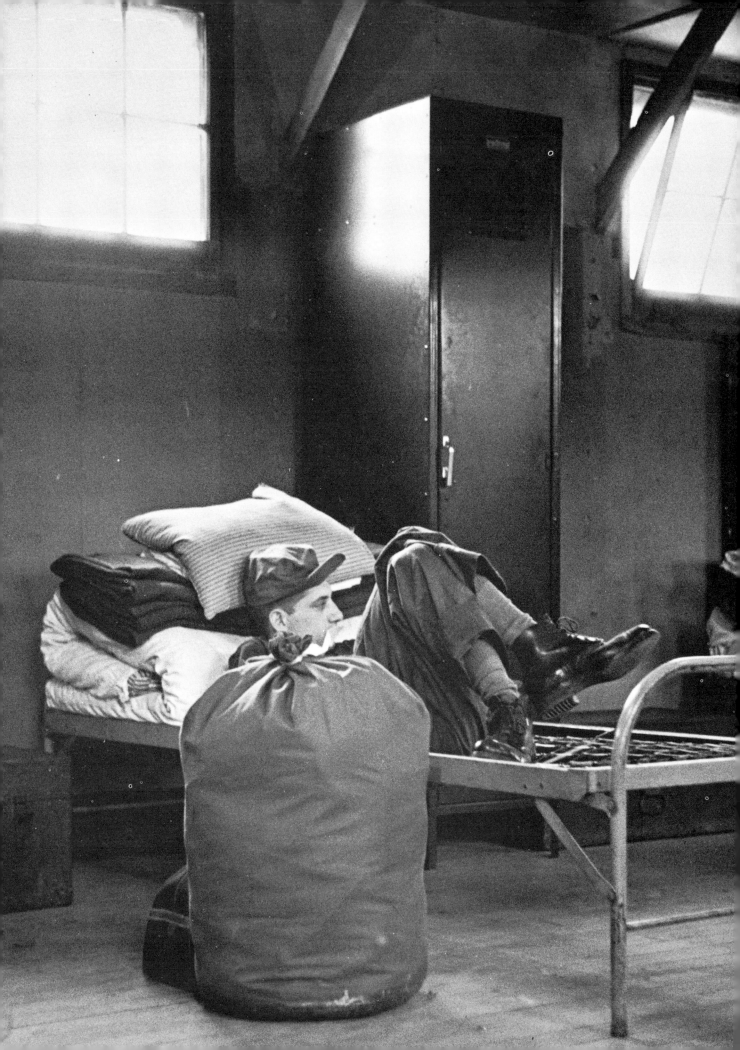

loneliness . . .

166

SOMETIMES CONFLICT LEADS
TO SERIOUS TROUBLE

Let me say at once that I do not believe in violence, and above all in the home. See this terrified little boy, standing in the corner, waiting horror stricken. Who is this strange man, this huge man, whom he had thought was a loving father, now changed into a menacing unknown? Yes, of course I believe in discipline, but this is not discipline. It is intimidation, the power of the big over the small, the powerful over the weak. The way of discipline is not this. The goal of discipline is the achievement of self-discipline and it can be reached only through the most careful, persistent, nonviolent teaching.

Violence does involve damage. A domineering, hot-tempered father, satisfying his own untroubled impulses, starts his child on the way to delinquency. The paroxysm of this small child, about to be whipped, sets up the train of violent acts which, later in life, would be the revenge he takes unconsciously upon his father.

It may not be the father. It may be an older brother or sister, who unless parents are alert, may be using violence to maintain a physical and emotional dominance. Whoever may initiate the evil sequence, the inhibited child is locked into withdrawal, from which he emerges only by seemingly inexplicable tantrums and rages. He may even run away from home and in adolescence, insecure and self-hating as he is, he may commit his own acts of violence in gangs and racial conflicts.

Nor is it always conflict. Insecurity and self-hatred may be expressed in an unduly strong desire to be accepted by one's peers, and in joining in the life of the gang to the extent of drinking, using dope, idle loitering in streets and bars, unhealthy admiration of one's fellows leading perhaps into homosexuality. Ah, that terrified little boy, cowering in the corner, waiting to be whipped, has more to fear than he knows! Yet the instincts which may lead to trouble are in themselves entirely normal. The need to be accepted by one's age group is natural and right, yet anxiety for acceptance may compel a boy or girl to repudiate the principles in which he has been reared, and even to reject his own family. He does this with a sense of guilt, for it is also natural to love his family, or wish to love them even when it manifests itself in defiance. What can parents do? It is not the time to press duty or obligation, for this only makes independence more necessary. Instead let us wait.

"I'm unhappy," a young daughter, home from boarding school, said to me the other day. "I ought to love my family best, but actually I feel closer to my classmates. I shouldn't, should I?"

"Of course you should," I told her. "And when you go to college you'll feel close to new friends. Don't worry. In due time you'll come back to a steady love for your family. They're your background, but all your life as you grow you'll be finding new friends. It's sad sometimes to leave old ones behind, but if they don't grow, too, it has to be done! 'Build Thee more stately mansions, O my soul' — remember?"

Guilt lifted, and this lively, growing creature went her way.

Others are not so fortunate. When the home is a slum and one's peers are gangs in warfare, the end is sure unless help comes. Sooner or later some will look at the world through prison bars, and the future, for a tragic few, may be death itself, for which even a good priest can scarcely prepare them. Oh, the awful loneliness of the young! The deepest tragedy in the world is contained in two words. "If only —"

Fortunately, most of our children are happy and good — normally good, that is, with only the usual ups and downs of growing up. Most of them do their best in school and live in reasonable accord with parents and brothers and sisters. Most of them manage their rebellions with increasing self-understanding. These we hear too little about and the relatively few others make news as the exceptions. The delinquents of whom we complain and for whom we suffer are a relatively small percentage of our total youth population.

Our hope is that our record will be even better, but we are all aware that this is a very complex problem. There are no easy answers. The heartening fact is that more than ever before people of knowledge and dedication are now concerned about our delinquent youth and about the many factors which contribute to their delinquency. We may take courage, for entire communities are working together to produce a more wholesome climate and better opportunities for these children, who need both our understanding and the most skillful services we can provide.

Most of our children, I repeat, by far the most, are worthy of our hope. We need them all. In this most challenging age of human history none can be lost. For who knows what brilliant scientist, what talented artist, is lost in a city slum or a sharecropper's shack?

terror . . .

WAYNE MILLER, MAGNUM PHOTOS, INC.

RALPH CRANE, BLACK STAR PUBLISHING CO.

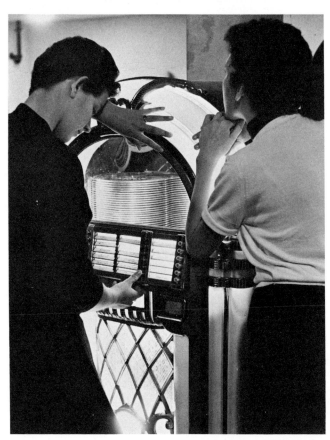

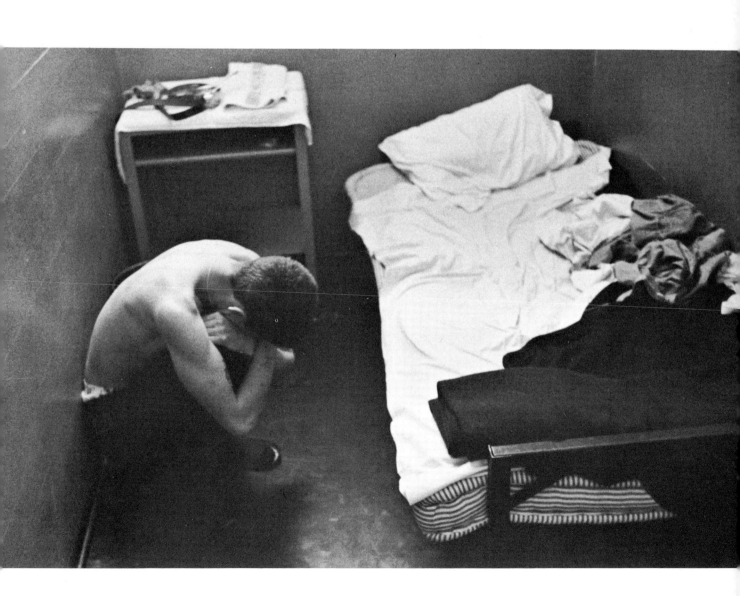

FOR MOST, THERE IS HAPPINESS TO SHARE

Surpassing all sorrows, except the most extreme, is the joy of being young and nature provides the joy. The flowing of young blood through healthy veins, the strong beat of the young heart, the awakening of the fresh young mind, the senses all alert, create together the source of joy, seemingly inexhaustible. It is the impulse toward life that holds back death.

And in what manifold and various ways youth expresses its joy in being alive! Jazz, incomprehensible sometimes to elders, seems to be the means of youth's expression, its off-beat, unpredictable rhythms suited to the searching, wilful moods of the young. Joy then is finding one's own kind in prep school and college dormitory life with its own language of catch words and jokes, joy too in sharing school life in our good public schools. Differences there may be of race, but happily youth does not think of race unless evil prejudice has been taught. Birthdays have a special meaning when one is young, and the presence of mother and grandmother emphasizes one's own youth and yet gives security to one's place in the generations. And of age, let it be added, not only the old define one's place but also the very young. A baby brother or sister is important because one sees one's self of only yesterday, loved and nurtured.

There is a wholesome wildness in the joy of youth, a madcap fancy, compelling laughter, but there is intense and sober concentration, too, as, for example, when one studies the fascinating intricacy of the engine in a car. An engine is made to go, it creates its own energy, and this in itself is an enticement to youth.

Above all, perhaps, youth is the joy in adolescence of knowing there are the others, the boys the girls, the girls the boys, those two magic parts which together make the human race. The knowledge begins vaguely in the home, where hopefully the good marriage, basic to happiness of the family, provides for the child the first awareness of love between man and woman. But this love, accepted for granted by the child, takes on a special individual meaning for the youth. He sees himself, she sees herself, separate from parents and family. Each becomes an individual through new love. It begins imperceptibly through the contacts of daily life in school, through work, through parties and play, making music together, in the band, horseback riding in the long summer vacation, walks in the woods. In every day meetings the new joy begins.

There are other joys, too, but somehow they all feed into the mainstream of the awakening of love. Girls chatter together at the soda fountain, seemingly to each other, but aware of the boy at the right who breaks in to tease while they pretend to ignore him. There is no need to ignore a football hero, woman. A girl can openly adore someone who wins a victory for the school. And a boy is a show-off for love's sake, a fool to draw attention to the all important self. And a girl makes a new dress in the home economics class to wear on a certain occasion. That is joy, too — to make a pretty dress. There are these individual joys, the joy of personal achievement which builds self-respect.

Youth is the age for joy. Let the cup overflow, let it brim over, for the years are short, the time is brief and joy is essential, I believe, to the future health, physical, mental and spiritual, of the human being. Just as childhood should be complete in family security and the opportunity for learning through play, youth should find completion through joy in life. Discipline but not restraint is the technique, discipline leading to self-management, and joy should be a part of that discipline. Indeed it is a very important part, for there is no greater joy in life than to know one has done well with one's self. Even love is more profound when it is expressed but under control. This, too youth discovers.

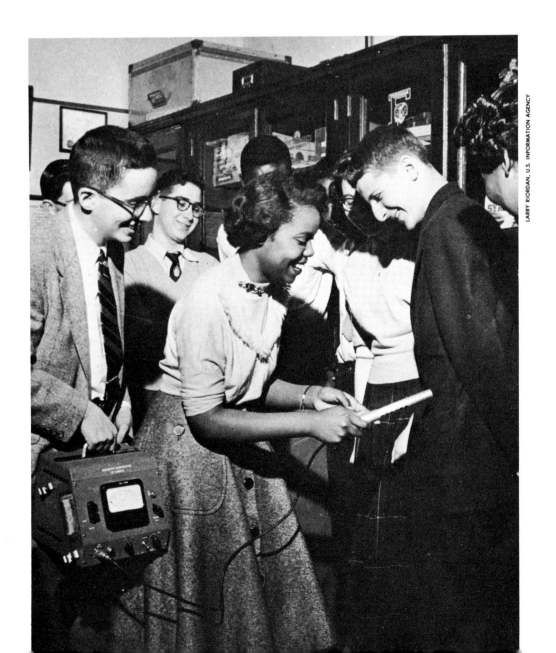

186

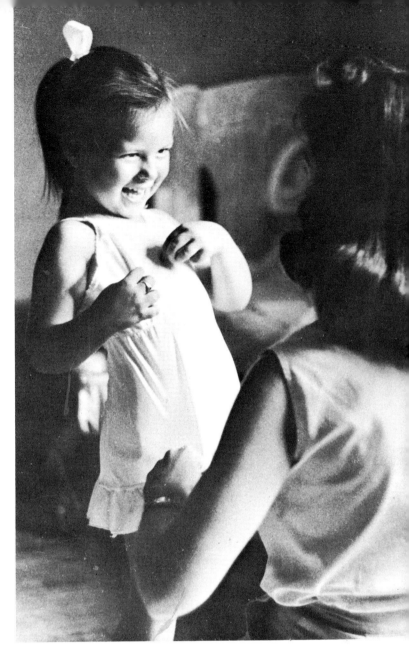

EVA BANKI

188

191

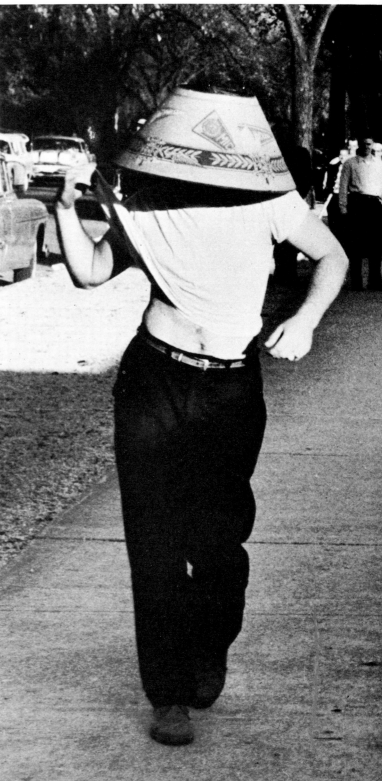

194

THIS IS YOUNG AMERICA—
OUR STRENGTH, OUR FUTURE,
OUR PRIDE

Our treasure is in our children, for in them is our future. And what a future! Ours is a pivotal nation in a new age. We may not wish to lead, but leadership is beyond our acceptance or rejection. Whether we will or no, whatever we do will mean leadership for other peoples. For ours is a history unique in all human history. From among every people and nation on earth our forefathers gathered or were gathered to this central continent. It was a virgin land. Old peoples live on the tired earth of ancient lands, they crop from dry grey soil their meager harvests. Ancestral shadows still warp their lives. But ours was earth fresh from the hand of nature. Forests had enriched our soil for unknown centuries and its fertility was and is unmatched. All that was needed to build a strong nation was here, and our forefathers, rebels in the ancient lands, were strong. We have no long dark history to cloud our present days. Whatever is dark, we made it dark by our own wrong actions. But there was always strength to oppose the wrong, and so far right has prevailed.

Will this right always prevail? The answer lies in the hands of our children. Do they inherit the strength of our forefathers? I believe they do. Will they be able to live their lives in such ways that they will lead the world toward a reasonable peace, a humane and universal prosperity, not by compulsion but by attraction? I believe they can — if, that is, they see the vision of what the world can be.

They cannot be expected to see the vision, I suppose, when those about them have none. I have myself seen no greater tragedy in my own country than the faces of young white people in our American South as they shouted their anger against their darker-skinned fellow citizens who for a hundred years have been deprived of their civil rights. Enraged, twisted young faces, hideous with cruelty! Who taught those young? And can they learn how dangerously wrong they are — can they learn in time to save themselves? What vision is theirs or can be theirs, unless they learn that all men are brothers, each with the rights and privileges of all?

Without vision, the prophet tells us, the people perish. The wealth of business, the comfort of life, the richness of the inexhaustible soil, provide no vision. Technology alone provides no vision. Vision comes from heart and mind working together to make dreams come true. What dream? The dream of a world where there shall be no more war, no more hungry people — half of the world's people today are underfed — where illiteracy is ended, where government is just and people are free.

This is the vision and our contribution to its final reality is our youth, our children reared in the security of love and home and the heritage of freedom. These are our best, our children, our strength and our pride. To the future we dedicate them, to the future of our nation and our world.

CAL BERNSTEIN, BLACK STAR PUBLISHING CO.

4-H CLUBS, U.S. DEPARTMENT OF AGRICULTURE

RALPH AMDURSKY, EASTMAN KODAK CO.

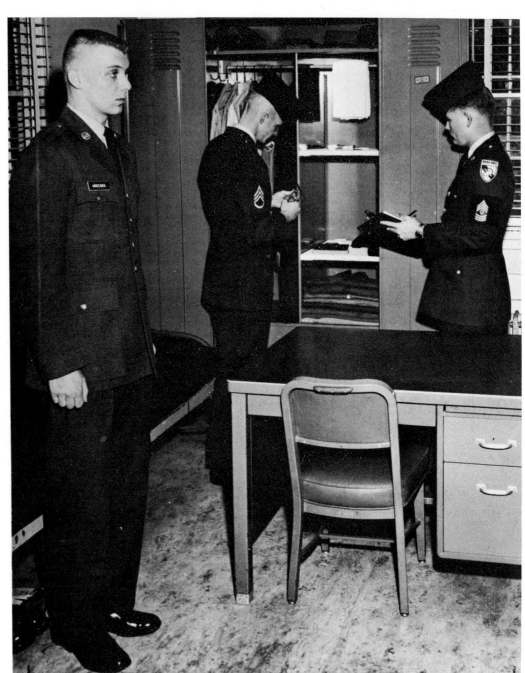

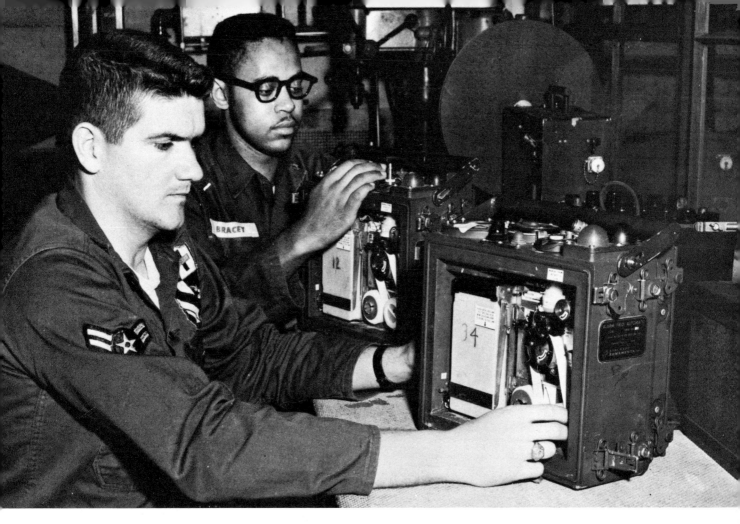

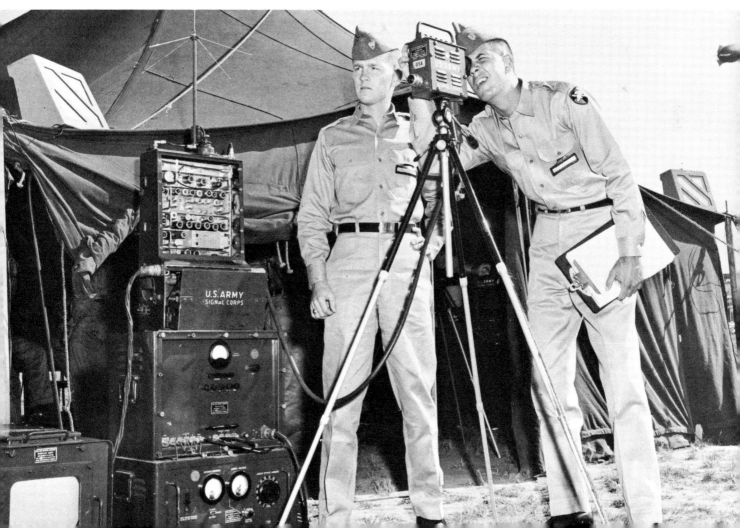

204

OFFICIAL U.S. NAVY PHOTO

OFFICIAL U.S. NAVY PHOTO

OFFICIAL U.S. NAVY PHOTO ON THE FOLLOWING PAGES

208

WASHINGTON POST PHOTO

JOHN AND BINI MOSS, BLACK STAR PUBLISHING CO.

WIDE WORLD PHOTOS, INC.

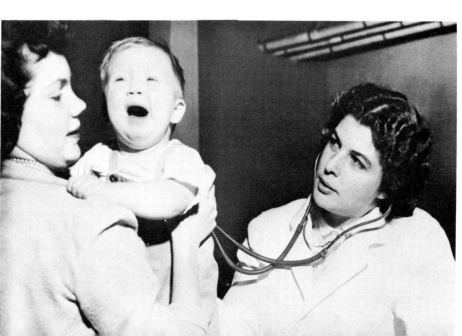

To the future we dedicate them, to the future of our nation and our world.